The Sermon on The Mount

Brief Meditations

by
James D. Rapp

*To all who have patiently endured my
teaching/preaching on the Sermon on the Mount
over the years – especially those whose responses
have extended and enriched my understanding –
to all of you I dedicate these words.*

Originally published serially on the Blog
The Cottage on the Moor

Contents

Introduction

As a very young pastor, in 1960 or some year shortly after that, I spent an entire year (fifty-two Sunday mornings) preaching sermons based on Matthew's text of the "Sermon on the Mount (Matthew 5-7). Those who endured that emersion were gracious to me, not complaining once (that I recall) about the content or the duration of that series of sermons. Of course a sermon is declarative device perhaps invented to dissuade all but the most bold – or the most offended – from accosting the preacher after the service is over.

In later years, when teaching adult classes based on Matthew 5 – 7, I did not always fare so well. My favored method of teaching has always been interactive so there was, in each session, an open invitation to disagree with the interpretation being offered. Though I did not always come to agree with the positions taken by my "tormentors" I always learned from them. They drove me back, time and again, to my "sources", especially *the Source*, the Word of God. One cannot return to this marvelous teaching repeatedly without acquiring a fixed notion that Jesus was deadly serious in all that he taught the crowd that day, and that we neglect those teachings to the hazard of our own souls.

We don't know how long the Sermon on the Mount lasted, nor do we know for sure in what form it was delivered. It is not called "The Sermon on the Mount" in the Bible. In fact, differences in the two accounts of it (in Matthew's Gospel and Luke's Gospel) have caused some discomfort to Bible scholars because Matthew identifies the place where it was delivered as being on a mountain, but Luke has Jesus going down to a "plain" to preach it. Matthew's well-ordered account of the sermon would lead us to believe that it was one uninterrupted monologue that could not have lasted more than fifteen or twenty minutes. Very likely the event on the mountain was a day-long adventure and Jesus teaching may have been distributed over the whole time, including the trip up the mountain and the trip back down again. It could well have been as much dialogue as monologue, with Jesus interacting with the crowd, responding to their questions.

The circumstances under which the sermon was delivered are interesting and not unimportant for some purposes, but it is the message that has captured the hearts and minds of thousands over the years, making the Sermon on the Mount, arguably, the most famous sermon of all time.

But the message has not failed to create controversy either. Modern Evangelical Christians, many closely aligned with or descendents of earlier Fundamentalist Christians, have been uncomfortable with what they see as the promulgation of a morality-based religion that ignores or, at the least, diminishes Christ's atoning work Calvary. The fact that the words are irrefutably those of Jesus complicates any attempt to dispute them so many Evangelicals have largely ignored, rationalized, and relegated them to "optional" status; nice things to see in a believer's character – things that need to be taught to children in Sunday School – but having little or no bearing upon one's standing before God.

The result of viewing the Sermon on the Mount, and Jesus' other moral teachings, in this way is that the purpose of Jesus' life as a man is reduced to miracle worker (to confirm his Messianic credentials), and sinless sacrifice for mankind. If Jesus' moral teachings are of little or no importance to the redemption of mankind, and if it were not for a number of Old Testament foreshadowings and prophecies that needed fulfilling, Jesus could just as well have died in Bethlehem with the other innocents. His miracle-laden birth would prove his Divinity, and his innocent death would provide all that is required for the substitutionary atoning sacrifice for mankind.

I believe the earthly, human life of Jesus meant something. He came to be what Adam failed to be. He came to feel what every human feels. He came to live under the curse of sin and temptation. He came to reveal the Father and describe the Father's will for the world we live in. He came to show us what life in the kingdom of heaven looks like; what a life focused on the Father and His will could accomplish. And, yes, he came to die and rise again, defeating death, the ultimate enemy. In his own bloody death he paid the price that would atone for the sins of all mankind. It is all part of the ***good news***.

So, all of Jesus' life has meaning and purpose, even his teaching on the mountainside. He was not describing some future (earthly or heavenly) kingdom in which men and women would *finally* live by the principles he described as "the kingdom of heaven." The kingdom was *here*, and *now*. John the Baptist had declared, "Repent, for the kingdom of heaven *is at hand*." Jesus declared the kingdom to be *in their midst*. He prayed to his Father, ". . . your kingdom come, your will be done, *on earth* as it is in heaven."

In the Sermon on the Mount Jesus was describing behaviors that those who became a part of his kingdom would display, not so much because they "learned" them, although he does speak of "practicing" them, but because they have become sons and daughters of God, brothers and sisters of the King himself, and kingdom living is the only appropriate way for followers – and especially brothers and sisters – of the King to live.

It is in the genetic makeup of children of God to be like their Father and like His Son. If they do not behave as their Father and His Son, it indicates one of two things: 1) they are not really followers of the King or, 2) there is a malady (a genetic anomaly?) that needs to be submitted to the King for remedying, lest it metastasize into a cancer and take the *life* of its victim.

In these meditations, originally written as daily entries in the blog, *The Cottage on the Moor*, no attempt was made be comprehensive as relates to the text of the Sermon on the Mount as recorded in Matthew, chapters 5, 6 and 7. Several subjects addressed by Jesus are discussed together because it seemed to me that the principle he was teaching applied to all of them. Likewise I chose not to annotate Scripture passages heavily. It is my hope that those reading the pieces will have read the Sermon on the Mount from Matthew's and Luke's Gospels and will be able to follow the chronological discussion I provide.

Most of all, my hope is that this discussion will inspire kingdom living, not because I believe such living qualifies one to have life everlasting, but because I believe it identifies those who have come to Christ in faith and have been granted eternal life. If enough of us begin living by kingdom standards – even imperfectly and sporadically – the world will have to take note of the fact that we have been with Jesus. When we have learned to live by them more perfectly and more consistently, some will see, and glorify our Father in heaven. And that is the purpose of our lives in Christ.

Chapter 1

The Best Loved, Least Observed Sermon Ever Preached

In my years of Bible teaching I've had no other portion of Scripture resisted as defensively as the Sermon on the Mount (SOTM). Those who came to class remembering those marvelous beatitudes – well, the early ones at least, before Jesus got to talking about persecution – found the sermon less to their liking for the remainder of chapters 5, 6, and 7 of the Gospel of Matthew. The common response to Jesus' blunt statements was, "I don't think he meant for us to take that literally." Or some might say, "You couldn't live like that in our world or people would walk all over you." But isn't that the point? Didn't they walk all over Jesus? Didn't he promise that they would walk all over those who follow him?

Evangelicals typically hold that salvation comes through faith in Christ alone, not through works done in the flesh. *I believe that.* Still we have these moral teachings of Jesus that seem to imply that there is some obligation upon those who wish to be approved by God to live righteously. He even went so far as to tell his audience that, unless their righteousness was greater than that of the champions of righteousness, the Pharisees, they would not enter the kingdom of heaven. The good Evangelical response to that is, "Ah, and Jesus was referring to his righteousness, which must be obtained through faith in him." *I don't believe that.* It is evident that his sermon was, in part, an expose of the hypocrisy of the Jewish leaders, but it was preached to "disciples," and he admonished them at every step to do better than the self-righteous Scribes and Pharisees.

Even the apostle Paul, to whom we Evangelicals like to run for grace when Jesus' sermons get too hot, lists a number of behaviors and activities which, if practiced, will, he says, keep one from inheriting the kingdom of God. On the positive side, Paul's list of the "Fruit of the Spirit" sound very much like the Beatitudes. And finally, Chapter 13 of 1 Corinthians could have as easily come from the mouth of Jesus as from the pen of Paul.

So what are we to do with this *Sermon on the Mount*? Is it, or is it not instructive of how one must live one's life in Christ if one hopes to inherit eternal life? I want, in the next several chapters, to explore Matthew 5, 6, and 7 and hope to be able to show that the righteousness Jesus declares to be essential is practical, day to day *right living*; for one to ignore it, and live beneath the righteousness of the Scribes and Pharisees, is to court disaster in one's spiritual life.

But I will give this much of a hint about my answer to the questions posed in the previous paragraph. I believe there is a difference between the requirements to get into the kingdom of God and those required to stay in it. In other words, you can't get in by good works. You won't stay in without them. Stay around and see where this takes us.

Chapter 2

The Sermon on a Flat Place On the Side of the Mount

Who is buried in Grant's Tomb? Silly question. Almost as silly, but not quite, as, "Where was the Sermon on the Mount preached?" Matthew's gospel clearly says that Jesus went up into the mountain where he spoke to his disciples; Luke's gospel describes him coming down to a "plain" where he preached to them. Who is right, and does it matter?

In some ways it doesn't matter. Matthew and Luke are presenting their inspired versions of the same event. Matthew was likely present at the event so he should be expected to know a mountain when he is on one. However, in chapter 4 of his Gospel, his description of Jesus' activities that preceded his preaching of the sermon is very generalized, apparently not intended to focus on much other than Jesus' general itinerary, leading up to the sermon itself. However, when he gets to his description of Jesus' teaching, Matthew's account becomes much more specific and voluble than does Luke's.

Luke apparently built his gospel from the remembrances of others. There is no evidence that he was an eye-witness to any of the events he describes in his Gospel. However, he introduces the sermon with a more detailed description of the "ordaining" of the twelve than Matthew does. It is obvious that each Gospel writer was inspired to draw from his own resources, according to his own interests and perceived purpose, the details he would used to tell his story.

"But," some object, "didn't the Holy Spirit inspire both Matthew and Luke?" Yes, I believe he did. "Then," the argument goes, "they cannot be contradictory."

This question requires us to pause a moment to look at the subject of "inspiration," a knotty topic on which I do not claim to have the definitive word, but do have some insights (inspirations?) to offer.

Luke's and Matthew's accounts may, in fact, not be contradictory; I believe they are not. But even if they were it would not negate the Holy Spirit's inspiration. Two persons can be inspired to write a description of an event – even have it published in a Christian journal – but they may not necessarily describe it the same way. They could even have opposing views of what happened. Inspiration doesn't necessarily guarantee accuracy. If it did there would be no need for four Gospels. One authentic, perfectly dictated record, would do.

No, inspiration puts the wind in the sails of the writer – sometimes starts the fire in his or her gut – but doesn't often dictate the specific details to be written. We hope it would prompt a desire to truthfully deliver what one knows; what has been revealed to one. While God inspired the writers of Scripture he obviously did not, except in some rare instances, dictate to them the things they wrote.

Luke gives us a very instructive description of how inspiration worked for him:

> Many have undertaken to draw up an account
> of the things that have been fulfilled among us,
> just as they were handed down to us by those
> who from the first were eyewitnesses and
> servants of the word. Therefore, since I myself
> have carefully investigated everything from
> the beginning, it seemed good also to me to
> write an orderly account for you, most
> excellent Theophilus, so that you may know
> the certainty of the things you have been
> taught.

To Luke inspiration often took the form of a task: 1) that "seemed good" to do, 2) for which he was well equipped, and 3) for which he felt there was a need.

Some have argued that Luke was the most pneumatologically aware of all the Gospel writers, recording, more than the others, the presence and work of the Holy Spirit. Yet he does not claim any special "anointing" or "inspiration" as he writes. He as much as said, "I feel compelled to write to you, Theophilus." He could hardly have chosen a more understated explanation for the writing his Gospel.

A careful reading of both Matthew's and Luke's Gospels shows them presenting essentially the same story. Jesus had just recently begun his ministry and large crowds were pressing around him seeking healing and deliverance from satanic powers. Jesus had attracted many, perhaps hundreds, of disciples. He seems to have sensed that it was time to single out a core group of disciples who would be most intimate with him; whom he could instruct and

11

empower to be the leaders of his church when he was no longer among them. To prepare for the selection of those who would be known as apostles, Jesus went into the mountain and prayed all night. It is instructive that Jesus sought "inspiration" as he approached the selection of his apostles. He knew that he needed to ascertain the will of his Father so that he would make the right choices. In the morning he selected the twelve whom he would call apostles.

After the designation of the apostles, Matthew's account describes him going (back?) up into the mountain to speak to his disciples. Luke says he went down to a plain to address them. The Greek word Luke uses is *topos*, a place, not necessarily a vast prairie. If one is to address a large group of people one needs a flat *topos* where the people can stand or sit and where the speaker can be seen and heard. Both Matthew and Luke are describing Jesus' search for such a place.

I don't personally think Matthew and Luke should have to reconcile their differing perspectives, but I can foresee a scenario where both are right. Jesus, we know, went into the mountain to pray all night. In the morning he came down and selected apostles. He then led all of his disciples up the mountain seeking a place where they could assemble to hear him preach. He needed a place large enough to accommodate the crowd but suitable for delivering a teaching, perhaps with surrounding walls of granite to contain and direct his voice. Looking back down the mountain he spied a large enough *topos* for his purposes and he led them down to it.

So it was there that he preached the Sermon *on a Flat Place* on the Mount.

I've spent some time establishing the kind of place in which Jesus may have delivered the teaching Matthew records in his Gospel. Still, knowing what he said there is infinitely more important than knowing the details of the place where he said it. We'll get to that soon.

Chapter 3

About Those Disciples

There is a lot of sloppy usage of the term "disciple" as it applies to those associated with Jesus. One can become confused by the way the term is used today. A disciple is simply a learner, a pupil, a follower. At times Jesus had hundreds, perhaps thousands of disciples. On one occasion he miraculously fed, with five loaves of bread and three fish, a crowd of disciples, numbering over five thousand, not counting the women and children present.

Today, however, when we hear the term, disciple, we are apt to think of the twelve men whom Jesus selected to be very close to him in life and whom, after his death, he designate to carry on the work he came to do. Those, we are told very specifically, he designated as apostles.

It is important to know who constituted that larger group of disciples who followed Jesus around Galilee and Judea, who were the target of his "Sermon on the Mount." and many of his other teachings.

In the case of the Sermon on the Mount, Matthew and Luke both describe large crowds coming to the region of Galilee from as far south as Jerusalem, from the north as far away as Tyre and Sidon, from the Decapolis west of the Jordon, and from all of Syria. No doubt most of those coming were Jews, but much of the territory from which they came was inhabited by Greek speaking Gentiles, and it is not beyond imagining that some of those in the crowds were either non-Jews or, at the least, proselytes (converts) to the Jewish religion. The distances covered – up to eighty miles or more – are astounding, considering that most traveled by foot.

The motives of those disciples were mixed. Luke and Matthew emphasize the healings and deliverances experienced at the hand of Jesus. Thousands, it seems, came to receive those blessings or to bring some loved one who needed the touch of Jesus.

We know that Messianic fever ran high in Israel at that time and undoubtedly a part of the crowd was hopeful that they had discovered, at last, the One who would free Israel from Rome's tyranny. There were Zealots even among the Twelve whom Jesus designated apostles.

But Jesus words, and the crowd's reaction to his words, indicate that many came, simply to hear him preach. No one in their time preached as he did, with such authority.

And, mixed among the crowds were those who were not disciples, infiltrators sent from the Jewish leadership in Jerusalem or from the local synagogues to discover who he was and assess the threat he posed to their leadership.

It was such a crowd that gathered into a flat place, a *topos*, on the mountainside to hear what has come be the most famous sermon ever delivered. For an ordinary preacher it would have been a heady

16

experience, seeing a crowd like that assembled from distances such as they had come. In our day it would be an occasion to videotape and broadcast it to the world in succeeding weeks and months. The sheer numbers themselves would suggest the power and influence Jesus could hope to wield on behalf of important causes around the world. It would be an event to replicate, time and again, on other mountainsides or other venues.

But this preacher knew himself and knew his crowd. He was not sent to build earthly kingdoms; not even earthly organizations. His apostles would never quite understand that, even to the bitter end. (Some modern day disciples still have not grasped it either.) But Jesus could not forget it. He knew as well that the crowd who relished the loaves and the fishes, and drank in his thinly veiled condemnation of Pharisaic religion, would evaporate when he began to talk of "drinking his blood" and "eating his flesh." So he never gave himself to the crowds, never sought to replicate his experiences, but daily looked to his heavenly Father to see what new thing *He* was doing.

But it was still early in Jesus brief, three-year, earthly ministry. The crowds were large and fervent, and mostly friendly. Jesus had a kingdom of which he wanted to tell them. Some would grasp it and they would be blessed. He did not dream of future, larger gatherings. Instead he viewed those few who grasped his teaching as a mustard seed that would grow into a large tree upon which the birds of the air would someday come and rest.

17

Chapter 4

Where are the Porta-Potties?

Before I can begin examining the Sermon on the Mount I need to know some important information. Like, where are the Porta-Potties located? *There are none*? This is going to require another miracle. Several thousand people gathered in a remote place, women and children among them, and no running water, no portable toilets available. What is this, a third-world event? Yes, it appears that it is.

I've been involved in the planning of large, community-wide, religious services – *involved in* mind you, not in charge of – and I'm astounded that Jesus would attempt to pull off something as big as the Sermon on the Mount without an advance team to line up support from area synagogues and get all of the logistics in place. I know it was a different time, and folks were more resilient and resourceful, but still . . .! Can't you hear critics whispering?

"I assure you there will be trouble if any kid gets hurt falling down the mountain. And that many people tramping across the countryside will leave a trail of debris that will give *Jesus Ministries* a bad name for years to come. I hope enough foresight was exercised to get the necessary permits for a public meeting of this kind. The Romans are ticklish enough about large gatherings without stirring them up unnecessarily."

It was indeed a different time and place where Jesus' ministry began and ended in three short years. He had no time or earthly resources for "advance planning." His Father in heaven had done all the necessary "advance planning." If things got desperate enough he would ask the Father and He would meet whatever needs arose. Bread or fish or wine could be available at his touch, not primarily to meet the short-term needs of a crowd, but that too of course. More importantly his miracles confirmed to the poor in spirit, the meek, those hungry and thirsty for righteousness, the peacemakers and the mourners, that they had come to the right place. No modern stadium, no modern event, no modern advance team was better prepared to meet the needs of the "multitude" than Jesus was.

Oh, are you looking for the Porta-Potties? There are plenty of them here. There is one just around that yonder rock. Be sure to rub your hands in the sand real good before you come back. Oh, and ask Sarah over there by the Porta-Rock if she has a spare loaf of bread that she could send back with you. Hurry now, the sermon is about to begin.

Chapter 5

Blessed Are the Poor in Spirit

The beatitudes are the best known part of the Sermon on the Mount, constituting for many, the entirety of what they know about it. The term, "beatitude," denotes a blessing, a gift, or even a title or office bestowed upon one. Each of Jesus' beatitudes begins with a "blessing" for those who meet the qualification that is paired with the "blessing."

Since many people have no trouble identifying themselves as "poor in spirit" or "meek" or a "peacemaker", or even perhaps "persecuted," it is natural to think of this part of the Sermon on the Mount as a wonderfully positive expression of God's benevolence. A perfect fit for one's own righteousness! That provides a false comfort as some of our further studies will show. But even if one gets through all the beatitudes feeling unscathed, that which follows – and that which makes up the greatest part of the sermon – is often anything but comforting if one takes seriously the words of Jesus.

Some of those listening to Jesus that day came, believing that, if only Jesus, or some other Messiah, would shake them free from the shackles of Rome, they would be living in the idyllic kingdom which God promised to David and his descendents in perpetuity. However, that day Jesus used a term that meant something very different. He spoke of a kingdom of (from) heaven. In other words, a kingdom among men in which the will of the Father would be done *on earth as it is in heaven*. Over and over the phrase, "kingdom of heaven," filled the sermon, emphasizing that the manner of living he was describing was the order of the day in the kingdom he proclaimed. Jesus would spend the next three years describing the character of that kingdom using one parable after another. They must repent of living in the old ways; the kingdom of heaven was at hand (in their midst) and they must learn how to live in that kingdom, with its new expectations.

It was, first and foremost, a kingdom for the "poor in spirit." All the kingdoms of this world are for the haughty in spirit. The winners in the kingdoms of this world are those with the largest egos, the greatest ambitions, the most self-confidence, the least concern for others. They are also those with the greatest sense of pique when their talents go unrewarded. Anyone foolish enough to defer to another's interest, another's wellbeing; to recognize another's rights, will go nowhere in the kingdoms of this world. If anyone who is poor in spirit is elevated, it is only allowed to happen because the haughty in spirit suppose they can find a way to benefit from allowing it.

But Jesus said, "Blessed are the poor in spirit, for theirs is the kingdom of heaven." The kingdoms of this world come and go, and some day they will go forever. But the kingdom of heaven is an eternal kingdom. The haughty in spirit have no place in that kingdom, nor do they want any place in it. The poor in spirit are comfortable there, thrive in it, and have the assurance that their investments in that kingdom are being stored as treasures that will not rust, or fade, or be taken away.

I believe Jesus started the Sermon on the Mount with this beatitude because it presents the essential character of the citizen of the kingdom of heaven. None of what follows in the Sermon on the Mount can be realized by one who does not possess – or is not possessed by – a poverty of spirit, a willingness to be last in all things, servant of all. Jesus says, here and elsewhere, that such persons will be first in the kingdom of heaven, not because they hope to be, or strive to be, or believe they have a right to be, but because God wills that they be.

Chapter 6

Blessed Are Those Who Mourn

Joy is the object, the goal, but we settle for happiness . . . if we can get it.

C.S. Lewis was right; joy cannot be gained by seeking it, only by being receptive to it, and perceiving it when it comes. Happiness, too, is difficult to come by. We lure it by stimulating our senses with sounds, and smells, and tastes, and sights, and touches, but find that it flees when the senses become accustomed to it, or grow weary of it. And so we spend most of our time "pursuing happiness," and only fleeting moments, enjoying it. Which is to say that much of our life – bereft of joy *and* happiness – is spent mourning their absence.

It is difficult to know for sure, the exact nature of the mourning Jesus spoke of in the second beatitude. He said, "Blessed are those who mourn for they shall be comforted." We get little help from the context of Jesus' statement but fortunately the same Greek word occurs in two other contexts in the New Testament and they give us some clue as to how the word might have been understood by those listening to Jesus that day.

The Greek word that Matthew uses for "mourn" is *pentheo*. The apostle Paul uses that word in 1 Corinthians 5. He chastises the Corinthian church because it did not mourn (*pentheo*) over the sinful behavior of a man in their fellowship living in incestuous adultery. Again in the second epistle to the Corinthians Paul urges the believers at Corinth to remove all sin from their midst so he will not mourn (*pentheo*) when he visits them.

These examples give us an idea of the kind of mourning Jesus had in mind as he spoke to the crowd before him on the mountain. He was offering the counterintuitive notion that those who were truly saddened – deeply sorrowful – about the sin and suffering around them were blessed. More to the point he was speaking of a sorrow over one's own sinfulness.

Unfortunate happenings trigger sorrow in nearly every person whether they are personally touched by them or not. A report of a natural disaster affecting thousands of people, or individual personal tragedies, can engender headlines around the world and inspire an outpouring of sympathy from those who have no personal connection to the event. Thus there are millions of "mourners" in the world at any given moment. Thank God that human hearts are capable of such compassion and generosity.

But sorrow for the sinfulness of one's society, or culture, or business, or family, is less common; often only expressed when it affects someone or something we value.

And sorrow for personal sin is arguably least common of all, unless one has been embarrassed by disclosure of their sin.

Jesus did not admonish his hearers simply to mourn; he pronounced them *blessed* if they did, and promised that they would be comforted. We must remember that he is presenting the perspective of the kingdom of heaven, not that of this world. According to this world's perspective the way past sorrow is a renewed "pursuit of happiness." Mourning is seen as an interruption of happiness. Don black for a month, lower the flag to half-mast for month, change your ways until society is no longer looking; then get on with living as you wish.

In the kingdom of heaven mourning is the way to joy. Who feels more joy than one wrapped in comfort? And it is comfort that Jesus promises to those who mourn. To mourn a tragedy and see it as a violation of God's intent for this world, to mourn the sinfulness of our culture and see the destruction it brings to those God longs to save, to mourn for one's own sinfulness, recognizing how it separates us from our God, is to act according to the principles of the kingdom of heaven.

Someday the kingdoms of this world will become the kingdoms of our Lord, but for now the kingdom of heaven exists in the midst of the kingdoms of this world. Jesus presumably could have taken his disciples with him when he left this world, but he intended them to remain as salt and light in this dark kingdom. Regarding his apostles, he prayed to the Father, not that He would take them out of the world but that He would keep them from the evil. Jesus said of his disciples, they would be in the world, but not of it; surrounded by the evil but not overcome by it, observers of the evil but not

27

rejoicing in it. On the contrary, they were to be mourning it.

Can mourning and joy co-exist? I believe they do. True mourning puts one on the side of God, living by kingdom principles. True mourners receive the comfort of God, assuring them that their broken heart is a reflection – even an expression – of God's own heart. What greater joy could a subject in any kingdom have than to know that they are perfectly in tune with the heart of their sovereign?

Blessed are those that mourn. Their reward is comfort.

Chapter 7

Blessed Are the Meek

When the prodigal son returned home his father welcomed him with an embrace, a new set of clothes, a feast, and a ring for his finger. All of those are symbols denoting his full acceptance into the family he had deserted. Presumably he was made heir again to his father's wealth though he had asked for, and been given, and had squandered, his share already. But his father sensed that he was a changed person now, humbled and imbued with a different heart.

Jesus was the inventor of that story. He painted a picture of the Heavenly Father as much as – or more than – a picture of the wayward, but then repentant, son. There is another son in the story too, a haughty, self-righteous man who resented any forgiveness shown to his wastrel brother. But the rejoicing in the household was for the restoration of the wastrel son, now transformed by remorse and forgiveness, and made an heir again of his father and joint heir with his brother.

The third beatitude emphasizes the attribute of meekness; Jesus said, "Blessed are the meek for they will inherit the earth." What is this *meekness* that Jesus blesses with the promise of possession of the earth? The apostle Peter, writing in his first epistle (chapter 3, verse 4), reminds Christian women that God highly prizes "the ornament of a quiet and *meek* spirit." So we are back to the character of one's spirit. Matthew speaks of "the king of Zion" coming, "*meek*, and riding on a donkey." Moses, the great leader of Israel, and giver of the Law, is portrayed as the *meekest* of men. Neither Jesus nor Moses were milquetoast pushovers, but they were unassuming and gentle of spirit; careful of the feelings of the vulnerable among them.

Again, we must remind ourselves that, when Jesus promises the earth to the meek, he is speaking of the kingdom of heaven. Those who wish to inherit the kingdom of this world will inherit, as well, the corruptions of this world. But there is a kingdom worth striving to inherit. And striving, in that kingdom looks nothing like striving in the kingdoms of this world. "Want to be greatest," Jesus will say. "Then be servant of all." That is absolutely contrary to the attitude and expectation of the world in which we live. In the kingdom of this world a quiet and meek spirit is seen as a sign of weakness, an invitation to be trodden on. But God "highly prizes" just those things that the world despises. Every prodigal who comes to him, meek and repentant, he will cloth in a rich robe of righteousness, and authenticate with a ring, declaring him to be an heir of the kingdom of heaven.

Poor in spirit. Mourning. Meek! With such God populates his "kingdom of heaven" on earth. Are these the kind of characteristics we can cultivate, making ourselves "fit" for the kingdom of heaven? I think not. But I believe they are the default characteristics of God's children. They describe our forbears before sin entered their lives and robbed them of those attributes that made them like their Father. Perhaps someday, somewhere, they will be second nature – no, *first nature* – to us again. Our problem now is that we bear the characteristics of the kingdom of this world and are thus unfit to live in the kingdom of heaven. We literally "do not fit" into God's kingdom. The message of John the Baptist, and later of Jesus himself, and still later, his disciples, was "Repent, for the kingdom of heaven is at hand." Repent of what? Of the attitudes of this present world, of course.

Those who truly repent of the attitudes of this world and seek to forsake them, will find that the Holy Spirit will quickly step along side them, willing to teach them those principles of the kingdom that Jesus spoke of in the Sermon on the Mount. And they will find the Father clothing them in the righteousness of his Son, authenticating them, and making them heirs and joint heirs with his Son of the very riches they so recently despised and squandered.

Chapter 8

Blessed Are Those Who Hunger and Thirst After Righteousness

Almost everything we long for is beyond our individual reach. They are not always unattainable, but almost always attainable only with the assistance of someone else. We want to be loved but there must be someone to love us. We want prosperity but in our economy our prosperity depends upon the fairness and generosity of others, or our ability to exploit the resourses of others. We want health but if we don't have it we can only hope for its return or seek those who can heal us. We want pleasure but, if we not to become narcissistic, it must be shared with others. It is difficult to think of anything the human heart desires that it can obtain, unassisted, for itself.

Except righteousness.

Jesus said, in the Sermon on the Mount, that those who hungered for – and thirsted for – righteousness would be filled. I suppose an argument can be made – some do make the argument – that Jesus was referring to the righteousness that is obtained only through faith in His sacrificial death, but I don't think, in this instance, he had that in mind. The Sermon on the Mount is a practical statement about life in the kingdom in which followers of Jesus live, the kingdom of heaven.

It is most certainly true that all our righteousness is incapable of making us worthy to stand in the

33

presence of a holy God. For that standing, we depend upon the righteousness imputed to us through our faith in Christ. But Jesus was talking about everyday right living; standing before our fellow beings, having a right attitude, speaking right words, desiring right things, standing for right causes, being "as we should be." And that practical, feet-on-the-ground righteousness, Jesus declared, is obtainable to those who want it intensely.

And who would not want righteousness? Well, honestly, most of us. Righteousness is one of those things we would like all others around us to have – to be. But we gladly and generously make exceptions for ourselves. Agonizing over, or sermonizing about, the unrighteousness of our world is not the same thing as hungering and thirsting to BE righteous. Jesus has already told us that those who mourn over the unrighteousness of the world will be comforted. Here, in this beatitude, he is telling us that citizens of the kingdom of heaven value righteousness enough to desire it *for themselves*. It is their food and drink.

When is the last time you heard anyone say, "Oh, more than anything else, I want to be fair, kind, generous, truthful, non-judgmental; I want it so badly that I can taste it!" You can be any or all of those things, simply by not being their opposite: unfair, unkind, ungenerous, untruthful, or judgmental. It requires action by no one other than you. In fact the actions of others – either persuasive or coercive – are impotent to make one be "as one should be." We become righteous (as we should be) by ceasing to be unrighteous (as we should not be).

But, human nature being what it is, we do not naturally, or easily come by the desire to be "as we should be."

God has graciously provided a way for us to be righteous in God's sight. Through faith in Jesus we can stand before God clothed in the righteousness of Christ. But it is God's desire that we live, in this life – in the kingdom of heaven – "as we should be."

How intensely do you desire to do that? Those who "hunger and thirst" to be "as they should be" can learn to "love mercy, do justly, and walk humbly before God." Those who "hunger and thirst for righteousness *will be filled.*"

So let it be, Lord. Your kingdom come, your will be done, on earth – in me – as it is in heaven.

Chapter 9

Blessed Are the Merciful

Are the beatitudes merely a series of truisms? Consider: "Blessed are the merciful for they shall obtain mercy." Isn't Jesus simply stating the obvious; those who treat others well will be treated well themselves? In a perfect world that would be the case. But then, in a perfect world all would treat each other well; there would be no consideration of doing evil to anyone; there would be no need to extend mercy to anyone. Evil would not exit.

But we live in the kingdom of this world. Evil does exit. Ours is a world so flawed that one might even be persecuted for having treated someone well. In fact it has often been so. In many regions on the planet, those who champion the rights of the underprivileged and persecuted find themselves persecuted, imprisoned or murdered for their good works. And even in a society as "civilized" as that in the U.S., to take up the cause of the poor and the disadvantaged is to risk being viewed by some, even in the Evangelical church, as naïve, or worse, as contributing to the general tendency of the "underclass" to depend, for its support, upon the charity of the hardworking in society.

However, in this fallen world, mercy has often been the only thing that saved the race from annihilation. South Africa, Argentina, and other places in our world could only find their way out of a spiral of recrimination and retaliation through a policy of forgiveness and mercy administered through councils of truth and reconciliation. Those efforts, especially in South Africa, were led by the church. How that must have pleased the heart of God.

Jesus hoped (and still hopes) to plant a kingdom of mercy within a our world; to seed this unsuspecting and un-God-conscious world with a healing salt that will staunch its bleeding wounds while it awaits the complete healing that will accompany His eventual return.

We haven't said much in our earlier discussions of the beatitudes about the "Blessed-ness" of those who live by the rules of the kingdom from heaven. Many translations use "Happy" instead of "Blessed." I'm not enough of a Greek scholar to know which word best captures the meaning Jesus intended. Is it possible that both are required to fully describe the beneficial effect of right living? Blessings are generally thought to be benefits gained or bestowed upon one; happiness is the pleasure of receiving and enjoying those benefits.

There must be some twisted pleasure in administering an eye for an eye; we amass enormous armies and expend millions of lives to extract the eyes of our enemies. But Jesus said there was pleasure and benefit to be had by showing mercy. Can we imagine what those might be? Perhaps the peace of mind from knowing we have not wreaked harm on innocents in our quest to make the guilty pay. Perhaps the relief in knowing that we will not need to spill our blood, or the blood of our loved ones, simply to perpetuate a cycle of eye gouging. Perhaps the ability to sleep at night without fear that someone is prowling in the dark, seeking to do to us as we have done to them. Perhaps the joy of having for a friend, one who most certainly would have been an enemy if we had not shown mercy. Perhaps knowing that by showing mercy we will be shown mercy, if not by our enemies, here, in this world, then for sure when we stand, naked of all true righteousness, clothed only in the righteousness of Christ, before the judge of all men.

It isn't always easy to know whether we are living by the rules of the kingdom of this world or by the rules of the kingdom from heaven. The rules of this world are not all bad; many of them have been patterned after the rules of the kingdom of heaven. And conversely, those of the kingdom from heaven are not always unmixed with this-worldly contaminants. But one of the surest evidences that we are citizens of the kingdom from heaven must be our willingness to show mercy.

In one of his dying acts upon this earth Jesus demonstrated mercy. Two men, hanging crosses near his, at first, taunted him, challenging him to show his Messianic powers by saving them all from death. But somehow one of the men experienced an epiphany. Amazingly, he saw Jesus, no longer as a common criminal on a cross, but as a future king. He said, "Remember me when you come into your kingdom." And Jesus, forgetting the abuse of the previous hours, seeing only the faith of the man, mercifully said, "Today you will be with me in Paradise."

Our words of mercy can be, as those of Jesus were, an invitation to enter the kingdom of heaven, to enjoy the only paradise we can know on this earth.

Chapter 10

Blessed Are the Pure In Heart

It is estimated that about three-fourths of our medical terminology has its origins (roots) in the ancient Greek language. The Romans, whose civilization followed, and to a large degree was Hellenized by Greek language and culture, simply carried the Greek terms over into their medical vocabulary, Latinizing the spellings where there was no Latin equivalent for a Greek character. Of course, Greek terms slip into our language in other areas than medicine, but with nothing like the frequency with which they appear in our medical dictionary. This all works to great advantage for the scholar of New Testament Biblical texts in that a great many words encountered in the Bible have already become quasi-familiar from other contexts. Often, those with no understanding of Koine Greek (the common language in which the New Testament was written) can hear the connection with modern usage when they encounter the Greek term, either spoken or in print form in a concordance.

Such is the case with the beatitude we study here, "Blessed are the pure in heart, for they shall see God." In this short beatitude there are three Greek terms familiar to modern medicine, *katharos (pure)*, *kardia (heart)*, and *optanomai (see)*. A cathartic is a medicine or a process to purge and purify some organ(s) of the body. Cardio is a prefix which, combined with other terms, describes aspects of the heart. Ophthalmology, of course, is the science of the eye and, consequently, of sight.

41

Jesus was not thinking medically when he said, "Blessed are the pure in heart for they shall see God." He was simply using the vocabulary of his day, but the juxtaposition of the words for "purity," "heart," and "sight" give us an opportunity to think of them in terms of their present usage. In purely medical terms the catheterizing (cleansing) of one's heart would not have any obvious or direct effect upon one's ability to see, or what they were able to see. So, in a literal sense, Jesus' words are nonsense.

In our day, though, just as in Jesus' day, the heart stands in for the mind and the emotions. Who knows where the mind and emotions really reside? Scientists are probing the brain, hoping to find the answer to that question, suggesting that human emotions, human motivations, and even human morality, may be nothing more that electro-chemical reactions in the brain. And what if they are right? Would it negate what we believe about humanity's special place in creation as the one creature made in the image of God? I think not. We've always known that the "heart" determines behavior. Jesus said that, "out of the abundance of the heart, the mouth speaks." A corrupt heart devises and speaks corruption. A pure heart devises and speaks good. The contents of the heart (its electro-chemical makeup, perhaps) is malleable. Jesus was appealing, in the Sermon on the Mount – not just with this beatitude, but through the whole sermon – for a change of heart, from one controlled by the rules of this world to one that is subject to the rules of the kingdom of heaven. And as an encouragement to seek that kind of heart purity, he promises that it will allow the one with a pure heart to see what those whose hearts are impure can never see, God Himself.

And how does a pure heart improve our sight? Jesus promised it would. He said, "They shall see God." It works in two ways: 1) by bringing the pure hearted into the kingdom of God where God is ever visible, ever on display in His Word, in His creation, and in the lives of other God-seekers, and 2) by the cathartic cleansing of the mind and emotions allowing the pure hearted to see the beauty of righteousness where before only self-interest was on display.

A clean heart sees God. There is, though, a part for us to play in this; we must want to see God. If that is our desire – our hunger and thirst – God's Spirit will teach us the ways of the kingdom, purifying the desires of our heart, allowing us to see God.

Keep reading in the Sermon on the Mount. You will find things there you wish you had, attitudes and behaviors you wish were yours. Hunger and thirst after them and you will be filled, and, being filled, you will see God.

The Sermon on the Mount will also reveal things you abhor in your heart and mind; attitudes, ideas, and behaviors that hide God from you. Allow the Spirit of God to remove them and you will see, in their place, the hand, and mind, and will, and face of God.

Chapter 11

Blessed Are the Peacemakers

There was a time when it was considered both appropriate and admirable for a son to follow his father in his life work. Not so much anymore, at least not in the individualistic cultures of the West. If anything, it is hoped that the son or daughter will "better themselves" by aspiring to a more prestigious or more lucrative vocation. It is hard to argue with that aspiration, especially when the child, by choosing a path different than their parent's path, is lifted out of poverty, or escapes from a health endangering occupation, or is delivered from a dangerous or corrosive family atmosphere. But there is still something admirable when a son or daughter sees value in the work their parent has done and decides to devote their life to continuing that work.

Jesus declared himself to be the image of his father. "If you have seen me," he declared, "you have seen the Father." So close was their will and purpose that he declared, "I am in the Father and the Father is in me." Jesus followed in his Father's footsteps: "My Father is always at his work to this very day, and I, too, am working." Theirs was a perfect union of purpose and work: "I tell you the truth, the Son can do nothing by himself; he can do only what he sees his Father doing, because whatever the Father does the Son also does."

Thus Jesus modeled what it means to be a son or daughter of God. It means to know the will of God and to make it one's own will. It means to sense when God is working, and how, and to what purpose, and then to devote oneself to being instrumental in all that God is doing.

So, what is God doing that His sons and daughters should be engaged in with Him? Many things, actually. He does not, however, require all His children to be engaged in all of them, or in any one of them all the time. But in one activity He desires all His children to be engaged constantly. That is the enterprise of reconciliation.

First and foremost, He desires that all humanity be reconciled unto Himself. The apostle Paul declares that all of God's children are to be engaged in the enterprise of reconciliation; to act as God's ambassadors, calling on men and women to be "reconciled to God." But further, the Father desires that men and women within His kingdom live at peace, and in harmony with one another. And finally He instructs us through scripture to live, to the degree that it is in our power, "at peace with all men."

Reconciliation has been the work of our Heavenly Father since the day that sin separated man from Him. It is God's will that all His children follow Him in His chosen work. It is hard work, and often the peacemaker does not get to see the result he or she would like to see. But God has not called us to be successful in all that we do. He has called us to be instruments through which He can reach out to those that are alienated by sin. Through His Holy Spirit He will make our peacemaking efforts as fruitful as they can be. We may be surprised someday to find that those cases we thought least successful have borne fruit we could not have imagined.

In no other way do we resemble our Father more than when we are peacemakers. In no other way do we bring more joy to the heart of God than by doing the work of reconciliation. There is rejoicing in heaven, Jesus tells us, when a single soul is reconciled to God.

Dare we believe that it makes the Father proud when He sees us doing the work of reconciliation? Could it be that our Heavenly Father smiles upon us when we are being peacemakers and declares, "There is my son; there is my daughter?"

Blessed are the peacemakers, for they *shall be called* the children of God.

Chapter 12

Blessed Are They Who Are Persecuted

Some debate whether verses 10 – 12 of Matthew, chapter 5, should be treated as a single beatitude dealing with persecution in general, or if they contain two beatitudes, one dealing with physical persecution and bearing the promise, for those thus persecuted, that they are a part of the kingdom of God, and a second one dealing with verbal abuse, bearing the promise of great reward in heaven. I will be treating them as a single beatitude, elaborated more fully than the others in Sermon on the Mount.

All of the beatitudes, and indeed all of the Sermon on the Mount, contain ideas that are counterintuitive, even contradictory, to the secular mind. They are, after all, kingdom ideas, descriptive of the values and ways of the kingdom of heaven. But none is more so than the teaching in Matthew 5:10-12 in which Jesus is quoted as saying:

> Blessed are they who are persecuted for righteousness' sake: for theirs is the kingdom of heaven.
>
> Blessed are you, when men shall revile you, and persecute y*ou*, and shall say all manner of evil against you falsely, for my sake. Rejoice, and be exceeding glad: for great is your reward in heaven: for so persecuted they the prophets who were before you.

It is important to note that Jesus did not promise the kingdom of heaven to all who are persecuted; only to those who are persecuted for righteousness' sake. Some would even argue that persecution for righteousness' sake is not, in itself, an indication that the persecuted one is in the kingdom of heaven. God will have to sort out those finer theological points. It is agreed here that being "hounded" – which, after all, is the sense of the word used in Matthew's Gospel for "persecuted" – is no sign of the rightness of one's cause. Even strong belief that one's cause is righteous is not enough. The kingdom of this world is rife with persecution of all kinds of people, especially any whose thoughts or conduct are a threat to those in power.

Here Jesus is speaking, not of a persecution that *puts one into the kingdom of he*aven, but rather of a persecution that stems from *being part of a kingdom, not of this world*; being hounded because one is seen as an alien in the kingdom of this world.

All of us have a natural desire to fit in, to be accepted in the kingdom of this world. If that is our goal then "ours will be the kingdom of this world." We can have what we want, but Jesus announces no "blessing" that accrues to those who attain their desired place in the kingdom of this world. There is no privileged "circle" in the kingdom of this world that will "bless" its members with contentment, happiness, or security. Only the kingdom of heaven offers *those benefits* to its inhabitants.

Persecution for the sake of righteousness does not confer the kingdom of heaven upon one, it confirms that one is a member of it, *and that confirmation is the blessing* – God's spirit bearing witness with the believer's spirit that he or she is a child of God.

Jesus went on to expand his description of the persecution that members of the kingdom of heaven will endure while living in a kingdom within a kingdom. It will involve verbal abuse, misrepresentation, name calling, and rejection. Again, the refuge from such treatment is an extreme joy that comes from knowing one is a part of the kingdom of heaven.

But there is a promise of an even greater, more eternal reward to come in heaven. Residents of God's kingdom within a kingdom have the hope and the promise that beyond this life the kingdom of God goes on. They will be a part of it; enjoying great rewards for all that they have endured for the sake of Christ and his kingdom. Like all those persecuted for righteousness in the centuries before – the prophets of Yahweh – they will enter into an eternal kingdom, the characteristics of which have not been fully revealed. One thing is for certain though; it will be a kingdom of righteousness, and those in that kingdom will be blessed.

Chapter 13

What Is This Kingdom of Heaven For Anyway?

The Beatitudes, and the rest of the Sermon on the Mount, make frequent reference to "the kingdom of heaven." It is not an easy concept to isolate and examine. As described by Jesus in the Sermon on the Mount, it represents the world the way God intended it to be. But it is more than a "spiritual" earthly kingdom, existing in the midst of a material one; it is a kingdom that encompasses all of creation. It has always existed, everywhere, and will exist to the farther reaches of eternity.

But the problem Jesus is addressing in the Sermon on the Mount is that another kingdom has intruded itself into the eternal kingdom of heaven, or at least that portion of it that encompasses our earth. And it is claiming to be the only kingdom there is.

Think of it this way. God established his sovereignty over all that He is and has made, but in one tiny part of that kingdom a revolt occurred; a counter-kingdom was established: the kingdom of this world – Satan's kingdom. God could simply destroy the rebel kingdom or He could try to redeem it. He has chosen to do the latter. The best way to redeem it is to reclaim it from within. So He has established a kingdom within the rebel kingdom for the purpose of saving that which He created and loves.

In the Sermon on the Mount Jesus presents the Father's plan for reclaiming that which is His by right of creation. Those who believe in His Son, and put their trust in him, will become representatives of His kingdom. Jesus used the analogy of salt and light to explain how this counter-revolution works. "You are the salt of the earth," he tells his disciples. "You are the light of the world."

Jesus himself came into the world to be exactly what he told his disciples they would be, salt and light. His life and ministry illustrated the manner in which his disciples would work to reclaim this world for God. "As the Father has sent me, so send I you," he told his disciples.

The two analogies that Jesus chose to describe the work of the kingdom of God are perfect pictures of the way his disciples would function in the world. Salt is passive. It can do its work of preserving and flavoring only in the place where it is. It has no motive force to carry it to another place. If it moves it is because the elements in which it exists are moving. If it is transferred from one element in its environment to another it is because those elements came in contact with each other. Wherever it is, or wherever it goes, it is always salt.

Light, on the other hand, is active, moving out from its source into the darkness around it, illuminating everything upon which it shines. Unless it is shielded or covered it will seek out something to reveal, something to shine on. As long as it is reinforced by new waves from its source, it will reveal the good and evil in its world.

Before we came to these words of Jesus regarding salt and light, we had just heard him list a number of attributes that describe the citizens of the kingdom of heaven. They are poor in spirit, mourners, meek, hungry and thirsty for righteousness, merciful, pure in heart, peace-loving. Despite these positive characteristics – or perhaps because of them – they are often persecuted. The persecution comes because they do not keep to themselves. They are not of the world, *but they are in it*, as salt and light.

Salt stings when rubbed into raw open wounds. Light infuriates when it reveals that which mankind wants to keep hidden. It would be so much more pleasant if God did not make his people salt and light; if they could simply be like the world they are in. But that misses the whole point of His plan to redeem the rebel kingdom. By making all who believe in him and trust in him subversive salt, and revealing light, God is retaking that which is His by right of love, by right of creation.

One by one, the salt heals those whose wounds have made them ready to be healed. One by one, the light finds those tired of the darkness. And so the kingdom of God grows.

Will we ever see the kingdom of this world destroyed? Perhaps not in our lifetime. But the day is coming, we are told, when the kingdoms of this world will become the kingdom of our Lord and of His Christ. Until then we serve as salt and shine as light. And we pray, as we have been instructed, "Your kingdom come, on earth as it is in heaven."

Chapter 14

Was Jesus a Rebel?

It was a law in Ancient Israel. Everyone washed their hands before they ate. There were signs above the lavatory in every Israeli restroom reminding all good Jews to do so. Well, okay! But there would have been if they had lavatories. And yet Jesus allowed his disciples to eat the grain from the fields they walked through without washing their hands. No wonder his detractors called him a Law-breaker. No wonder he was required to defend himself and his disciples: "Do not think that I have come to abolish the Law or the Prophets; I have not come to abolish them but to fulfill them.

In fact Jesus declared in the Sermon on the Mount that his disciples' righteousness needed to exceed that of the champion hand-washers, the Pharisees and the teachers of the Law, if they wished to be a part of the kingdom of heaven. Further he declared that not the least accent mark within the Law would pass away until it had been fulfilled. To break the least of the laws and to teach others to do so made one "least" in the kingdom of heaven.

On the surface it might appear to a casual reader that, in the rest of the Sermon on the Mount, Jesus often contradicted his claim. Over and over he would say, "You have heard it said . . ." and then go on to proclaim a need for his followers to do something different than, or more than, that which they had been taught the law required.

Murder, adultery, divorce, oath-breaking, retribution, are things they had been told they should avoid as good Law-abiding Jews. Jesus did not dispute the evil of those sins, instead insisting upon a standard of righteousness that "exceeded" that which they had heard from the Pharisees and the teachers of the Law.

At first it may seem a relief to hear murder equated to hatred, adultery compared to simple "lustful looking," retribution replaced with non-violence. But eventually it dawns on one that the "kinder, gentler" standard not only is no easier to achieve, but failure to live up to it has immediate and eternal consequences as serious as failure to keep the Pharisaic code.

So, why is this "good news?" Why did these people hear Jesus gladly? Why did they travel many days journey to hear his Sermon on the Mount? Hope, undoubtedly brought them. Desperation too. Curiosity. Diversion. All the reasons that draw crowds to hear charismatic speakers today.

Was this really good news? In a sense, no. Jesus was not offering an easier way than that offered by the kingdom of this world. Almost all of those who followed him early in his ministry drifted away by the time he reached the cross. It was too steep a grade for their feeble feet. The standard Jesus offered as the pattern for living in his kingdom was more impossible than the one the Pharisees imposed upon the people.

The good news was that Jesus did not expect them to achieve this righteousness in their own sin-diminished strength. He came to offer something more than a plan for moral living. He came to give himself – to break the grip of sin upon the human heart. He told those who came to him, and believed on him, that they would have, flowing from them, "rivers of living water." The Holy Spirit would be in them, and alongside them, teaching them, and prompting them to live like citizens of the kingdom of heaven. And when they failed – for they would certainly fail – the same Spirit would draw them back to the Father with the promise of forgiveness.

Jesus was no rebel. He was no Law-breaker. He was the faithful Son, revealing the true meaning of the Law and fulfilling the promise of the Prophets. True, he did not insist that his disciples wash their hands before eating grain plucked from the stalk; he insisted, instead, that their whole being be cleansed by the blood of his sacrifice. He knew that kingdom living came not from dogged determination to master a set of rules but rather from a heart cleansed of sin and in love with the One who cleansed it.

The "rules" of the kingdom would mark the behavior of those who chose to be a part of the kingdom of heaven, but they would be the product of a life yielded to, and directed by, the Spirit of God.

Chapter 15

Worship Indeed, But Make it Real

In the first third of the Sermon on the Mount Jesus: (1)laid out the characteristics of the citizens of the kingdom of heaven (in the Beatitudes), (2) described the role his disciples would play in the kingdom of the world (acting as salt and light), (3) explained his relationship to the Law (he came to fulfill it, not destroy it), and (4) refuted the rigid but shallow understanding of the law that the Pharisees and teachers of the Law were enforcing.

In Chapter 6 of Matthew's Gospel the sermon takes up issues of the heart, beginning with sincerity of worship. Jesus contrasts appropriate worship with the showy and hypocritical worship of that day. The picture Jesus draws of prayers offered on street corners, of trumpets blaring as offerings are brought to the temple, seem exaggerated. Is Jesus creating a caricature of the Pharisees' worship for purposes of making a point? It is tempting to believe he is. The religious icons of that day set themselves up for such treatment. But what ordinary person would dare make light of the sacred men and their time-honored practices?

Religious expression in our day has become, if anything, more public, and more showy, than it was in Jesus day. Granted, street preachers do not fare well in our secular society; they are often ignored or ridiculed in western culture. However, the equivalent of the proud and public Pharisee can be seen today on the television and in large auditoriums and stadiums around the world. Many ordinary Christians, looking on in bewilderment, wonder if they have the right to question the piety, the sincerity, the spiritual legitimacy of these champions of worship, prayer, preaching, faith, health, and prosperity.

Righteousness, as portrayed by the Pharisees, in Jesus day, or by the paragons of performance of our day, is beyond the reach of ordinary people, not because it is a righteousness, more lofty, more difficult to achieve. To the contrary, it lacks, in practice, what ordinary people believe real righteousness should have, solid sincerity. The righteousness of the exhibitionist requires one to stoop to behaviors most would not employ in the ordinary pursuits of their life. Onstage, among fellow religious revelers, it looks good, sounds good, feels good, has a reputation of being good. Often it even evokes, in some observers, admiration and a desire to emulate it, but when most try it on, it just doesn't fit. It is a flashy suit hiding a hollow man or woman inside.

The crowds that heard Jesus' Sermon on the Mount were glad to hear someone strip away the hypocrisy of such "righteousness" and reveal a way that *everyman* could worship their God.

Charity (support for the poor), prayer, and fasting were, Jesus taught, a matter between the individual and God. The left hand had no need to know what the right hand was giving. That was between the right hand and God. The neighbors did not need to know that one was praying, it was a conversation between the supplicant and God. Nothing was added to the value of a fast by making it known through a gaunt, disheveled appearance. It was a time set aside to better know God.

It is the tendency of religious institutions and professional religious leaders to systematize the behaviors of piety that are required of the "righteous." And it is the tendency of some to specialize in those behaviors, elaborating them, magnifying them, institutionalizing them, popularizing them, and eventually, packaging and profiting from them. They become the hallmarks of righteousness. Along the way the kingdom of heaven begins to look, and sound, and feel, not much different than the kingdom of this world.

Jesus' Sermon on the Mount showed the ordinary citizen of the kingdom of heaven a way around all that clutter, to a "closet" of real intimacy with God. In a few short phrases he captured the spirit of "rightness" that should embody all of our dealings with God and man. We'll look at that next.

Chapter 16

The Model Prayer: Teach Us How to Pray

The prayer we call "The Lord's Prayer" is recorded by both Luke and Matthew. Matthew, in chapter 6, places it in the context of Jesus description of the showy prayers of the Pharisees. Luke frames it in a different context. He tells us, in chapter 11 of his Gospel that, after observing Jesus praying, his disciples requested that he teach them how to pray. Though the details vary from Gospel to Gospel we get essentially the same teaching in both instances.

Although the lessons we take away from this "example" prayer is the same whether we are considering it from Matthew's account or Luke's, it is important to keep the context of Matthew's account in mind. His immediate audience was a large group of "disciples" who had come from miles around to hear him teach. But also present were the Pharisees, if not in person – though they very likely were there in person – at least they were in the thoughts of Jesus and his hearers. The Pharisees were champions at prayer, and at every other display of "righteousness." Still no one asked them to teach the disciples to pray that day.

Jesus' model prayer was nestled in the midst of his critique of the prayers of the Jewish religious leaders. His model prayer is meant to contrast with their prayers, which were public, and showy, and consisted of long repetitive recitations thought to make them more meaningful through sheer force of their verbosity.

By contrast, Jesus model prayer, with the sparest of words, focuses on five things: 1) recognition of God, the Father, and worship of Him, 2) a wish that the kingdom of heaven would come and that it would be as effective on earth as it is in heaven, 3) a prayer for daily needs (bread), 4) a request for forgiveness of sin and a reminder that we must forgive those who have harmed us, and 5) a prayer that God will protect us from the evil in the world.

Bear in mind that this is a model prayer, not intended, by Jesus, to become a liturgical piece, repeated until its meaning was lost as thoroughly as was any of the meaning that might have once existed in the prayers of the Pharisees. "This, then is *how* you should pray," Jesus said. Not *what* you should pray but *how* you should pray. Even the categories of concern listed in the previous paragraph are merely illustrative of what might go into a prayer.

Undoubtedly the aspect of Jesus' prayers that caused his disciples to ask him to teach them to pray was the sense they gained, watching and listening to him, that he was really talking to someone who, in turn, was really listening. The example Jesus gave them models a conversation in which the one praying makes contact with another One whom he trusts and respects; One he believes will do the simple, practical things he asks. The requests are framed to consider the will of the One being petitioned. They address the concerns of daily living as citizens of a kingdom within a kingdom: i.e. the barest needs of the supplicant, a concern for reconciliation with others, and a desire to escape the contamination of this world's evil.

Those foci will not always represent the content of the believer's prayers, but they catch the spirit of genuine prayer. Prayer, as represented by Jesus, is unpretentious, practical, God conscious, trusting, other-ward, and sincere. It will look and sound different on different tongues. Its content and character will be shaped by its context, sometimes quiet, sometime urgent, sometimes shaking the place in which it is prayed. There will be those who seem to be "better at it" than others – the fervent prayers of righteous men and women will seem to avail more than the prayers of others. But it should never be Pharisaic, pointing to, and elevating, the one praying.

We all should be "better at it." The fact that Jesus accepted the offer to *teach* his disciples to pray seems to say that it can be learned, and if learned, then learned to a greater or lesser degree.

Lord, teach *us* to pray, to pray well and often, and to glorify You in all that we pray for, and pray about.

Chapter 17

The Eye Is the Light of the Body

Jesus healed many blind persons in his three years of ministry on earth. Those miracles of healing undoubtedly served various purposes: defeating the work of Satan, bearing testimony to Jesus Messiahship, extending mercy to the suffering. But they also were an indication of his desire to open the spiritual eyes of those blinded by the lies of Satan and the deadening influences of the kingdom of this world.

Jesus was not a scientist. The pre-existent Son of God gave up his omniscience and came into human history as the son of man, required to learn and know what other men of his time learned and knew. The world he saw through human eyes was the same as that which his disciples saw. What he learned, beyond the knowledge and wisdom of his contemporaries, came as a result of his attention to the world around him, his mastery of Scripture, and his keen ear attuned to his heavenly Father. He availed himself of spiritual insights, available to, but seldom accessed, by other men and women of his time.

The illustrations and analogies he used to drive home his teaching were those that were the currency of that time. When he spoke of the eye as the source of light for the body he was drawing upon a common assumption about the way eyes function. We have a different understanding today, knowing what biological and anatomical studies have shown us. But the analogy of the eye as a source of light for our body still works today. Jesus said:

> The eye is the light of the body. If your eyes are good, your whole body will be full of light. But if your eyes are bad, your whole body will be full of darkness. If the light within you is darkness, how great is that darkness!

Jesus surely knew that the eyes were not the only source of "light" for the body. He knew, as well, that the "body" of which he spoke represented man's consciousness. All the senses contribute information that enlightens the mind, and the mind, in turn, instructs the senses, training them to seek, and apprehend, and value certain inputs and reject others. It is the mind (sometimes called the heart, by Jesus) that determines if the "eye" is good or bad; whether it serves to bring light or darkness into person's life.

All of our senses can be damaged, plunging us into a "darkness" that deprives us of the sights, sounds, touches, tastes, and odors available to us. But Jesus was not talking about physical impairment, though the incidence of blindness in that day was great enough that his audience would immediately connect with his illustration. It was a dulling of all the spiritual senses that Jesus was speaking about. Inordinate desire for sensual gratification of any kind can eventually deaden our sensitivity to, and hunger for, the good things of God's creation.

The eyes and ears, more than the other physical senses, are most informative about the world in which we live. Much of what we take in through those sources comes, virtually pre-loaded with meaning, requiring little processing before it affects our thoughts and actions.

Jesus chose to single out the eye as the source of light for the body, allowing it to stand in for all the senses that inform us, physical or spiritual. If the eye – a.k.a. the senses – is trained to admit good things for our consideration, our whole being will benefit and, to use Jesus' words, be filled with light. But if the eye is corrupted; if it reinforces the darkness that is latent in all humankind – pride, lust, greed, selfishness – the darkness in us will only deepen, making it less and less likely that we will ever be drawn to the kingdom of light to which God calls us.

All of our senses require training, and there are two tutors standing ready to offer us their services. The most popular tutor requires the least up-front investment, in fact advertizes that his services cost nothing, but his record is abysmal; all of his clients, without exception, have ended blind. Only with the services of the second tutor have any of them managed to reclaim their sight. Sadly, few of those blinded, seek restoration. The majority, believing they are not blind at all, but rather filled with light, continue to take in the darkness they have come to depend upon, all the while calling it light.

The second tutor requires a payment, up-front, of all that you have, and all that you are. But he will tune your "eyes" – if you let him – so finely that you will be able to sense and participate in every legitimate joy available to man, here on this earth, and through all eternity. Jesus is his name. He is the one who said, "Blessed are the pure in heart, for they shall see . . ."

Indeed! They shall see God!

Chapter 18

Do Not Worry About Tomorrow

What hiker, setting out to walk the Appalachian Trail, would fill his or her pack with the supplies needed for the entire trip? None, of course. A reasonable person would take what he or she needed to get to the next supply stop on the trail and no more. Anything beyond the necessities would, at best slow progress and, at worst, result in failure to complete the course.

In the Sermon on the Mount, Jesus concluded his admonition to his listeners concerning worry about the necessities of life by saying:

> Therefore, do not worry about tomorrow, for tomorrow will worry about itself. Each day has enough trouble of its own.

It is hard not to imagine a smile on Jesus' face as he said those things. He is playing, wonderfully, with words. He tells his listeners that they do not need to worry because the day itself will worry for them. Of course days don't worry; they only provide the context in which humans worry. Then he goes further and suggests that it is possible to reach ahead into a coming day and transfer its worries to the present one. How foolish, when we can't know how many of the concerns of the present day are worthy of worry, to assume that we can select future concerns that need our attention now.

Jesus had been preaching about the evils of what we might call materialism. But it was more than that; it was a materialism mixed with faithlessness. At one point he stopped to exclaim, "Oh you of little faith." It is important to pay attention when Jesus uses that phrase. Some have assumed that faith has degrees ranging from a little bit to a great deal. Although Jesus speaks of "little faith" and "great faith" it becomes obvious that "little faith" is inadequate to accomplish anything. Only "great faith" moves mountains. And only "great faith" believes God to supply one's needs each day. "Little faith" says, if I can build great barns and fill them I'll be able to rest easy for the rest of my days. "Great faith" looks no farther than the present; it says, "Give us, *this day*, our daily bread."

Jesus does not suggest that the lilies of the field, or the sparrows, are provided for because of their faith. He cites them as examples of God's care for the least of his creatures. Observing such care, we should have no doubt that he will care for us.

The pagans – who, by the way, live in the kingdom of this world – concern themselves with the amassing of food and drink, and clothing because they do not know what the children of the kingdom of God know. Children of the kingdom of God know that He has all their needs covered; that he even has the hairs on their head numbered. They are free to "seek first the kingdom of God and God's righteousness" knowing that all those things the pagans run after, will be given to them.

None of this is to say that one cannot – or should not – plan for the future. Hikers would be foolish not to have researched the trail they plan to hike, to decide how far they hope to go each given day, where they may stay each night. What they should not do is spoil the joy of their present moments by worrying if the provisions they have made will be sufficient. If we are diligent and faithful in our preparations God will faithfully see to it that they meet our needs.

So, fellow hikers, as you fill your backpacks for the next day's journey, pack just enough to get to the next way-station. There will be a new supply waiting there. And if there are unexpected needs along the way, trust that the one who planned the excursion can provide all that is needed to get you to your destination safe and sound.

There is a special bonus for those who pack lightly and trust greatly. They have more energy to expend exploring the wonders of the trail, seeking first the good things, knowing there will be enough of the necessities to keep them going.

Chapter 19

To Judge or Not to Judge: That Is the Question

Don't you just hate it when someone speaks out of both sides of his or her mouth, seeking, it seems, to be on all sides of an issue? One moment you are shouting, "Amen!" to their first proposition. The next moment you are bewildered, wondering if you should be affirming their equally fervently stated, but apparently opposite opinion on the same issue.

Possibly, those listening to the Sermon on the Mount found themselves scratching their heads when Jesus seemed to be saying opposite things about judging others, first admonishing against judging others, then urging his hearers to judge the fruit of false prophets. A little careful reading and some reflection will help us get around the seeming contradiction.

First we need to realize that living *is* judging. Consciously, or unconsciously, living creatures never cease, at least in their waking moments, to make judgments about the environment in which they exist and, to the best of their ability, adjust to it for their safety, comfort, and long-term viability. That process seems to go on from the simplest amoeba or sapling to the complex organism we call "man". So, *judging* is a natural and necessary process.

The judging that Jesus speaks of, which Matthew records for us in chapter 7, verses 1 – 5, is of a different character than the natural and necessary process spoken of above. Jesus is speaking of a tendency of humans – perhaps humans uniquely among all creatures – to judge others for purposes unrelated to improving one's own condition or assuring one's survival. He really had the Pharisees and other self-righteous leaders of his day in mind. They were quick to see the "speck" in their neighbor's eye and point it out while ignoring the "plank" in their own. Jesus called such *judging*, hypocritical, and promised that those who engage in it will, themselves, be harshly judged.

It may not be so much the "seeing the speck" in the brother's eye that Jesus condemned, as the inability to "see the plank" in one's own eye. After all, it is sometimes a favor to a "brother or sister" to point out the piece of lettuce wedged between their teeth. But one needs to then ask, "How do I look, brother? Can you help me improve?"

Mostly, though, Jesus is concerned about the underlying motive of the one judging. In the case of the Pharisees, the purpose was to diminish the status of the one they criticized in the hope of making themselves appear more righteous. That kind of judging Jesus firmly condemns:

> Do not judge, or you too will be judged. For in the same way as you judge others, you will be judged, and with the same measure you use, it will be measured to you.

Later in the sermon, Jesus returns to the subject of judging. Matthew records his words in chapter 7, verses 15 – 23. Jesus begins his remarks by saying:

> Watch out for false prophets. They come to you in
> sheep's clothing, but inwardly they are ferocious
> wolves. By their fruit you will recognize them.

These are strong and fearful words. In this case
Jesus lays upon his disciples the *responsibility* of
judging others who make a profession of being his
followers. It is a fearful responsibility because it
entails a judgment that affects the "safety, comfort,
and long-term viability" of the one doing the
judging, making him or her subject to the same kind
of scrutiny with which they judge another. Equally
awe-full is the realization that such judgment may
have negative consequences for – may damage the
reputation of – the one being judged. We dare not
be wrong in labeling others "false prophets." And,
since we live in community with other believers our
judgments may well affect the few or many who
attend to our opinions. Great harm and disruption
can accrue to a community of believers when
accusations of "falseness" are made irresponsibly,
or in error.

But still, we are admonished, by Jesus, no less, to be
on the watch for those who say, "Lord, Lord, didn't
we do marvelous things in your name?" but of
whom he will ultimately say, "I never knew you."
The final judgment of false prophets will be the
Lord's to declare, but we have a responsibility to
guard against them for the sake of our own souls
and the souls of those we love.

We have not been left without a measure by which
to judge them. "By their fruits, you shall know
them." Some simple questions can help us. Who
benefits – financially, and in any other way – from

79

their "ministry"? Who receives the glory for their lives and the things they do? Do they look like, sound like, live like Jesus? Does my spirit, instructed by the Word, and guided by the Holy Spirit, say "amen" to what I see them doing, hear them saying, and know them to be.

Most of the time we can judge quietly, and make decisions – to "endorse" or not "endorse" – that are privately held. But there are times to speak openly; times when, not to do so, allows those for whom we have responsibility to be drawn into error or, in some cases continue in error.

In summary, to paraphrase Jesus' teaching on judging, "Don't be picky about your brother's or sister's faults; you ain't perfect yourself. But don't be fooled by wolves in sheep's clothing, either. Not everyone who says, "Bah! Bah!" is a sheep."

Chapter 20

Dogs and Pigs

Jesus has a reputation in some circles for being "meek and mild." Meek, at least, is one appropriate descriptor of Jesus. But "mild" he was not always.

Jesus was always a presence, wherever he was. And his pronouncements regularly challenged those to whom he spoke. He uncovered hypocrisy by identifying the motives of his hearers; showing that their righteousness consisted of a legalistic observance of the external aspects of the Law while, at the same time, avoiding its essential requirements. He frequently used strong language in describing those whose religion had become an empty shell, calling them whitewashed graves housing the remains of dead men.

Some heads must have turned when he said, "Do not give dogs what is sacred; do not throw your pearls to pigs." Who are these dogs he speaks of? Who are the pigs? Jews of Jesus time were despised by their Roman overlords and they returned the hatred in kind, referring to the Romans as Gentile dogs. Pigs were an unclean animal to Jews as well, providing a ready epithet applied, as well to Gentiles. Did Jesus have the Romans, and other Gentiles living among the Jews, in mind when he spoke of dogs and pigs?

And what are the "pearls" that should not be cast before swine; what are the sacred things that should not be given to dogs? Were the Jews in the habit of distributing prayer shawls to Roman soldiers? Did they regularly operate vacation bible schools aimed at converting Gentile children? Was Jesus opposed to friendly interaction between Romans and Jews?

These are not easy questions to answer. Certainly the language Jesus chose to use would have turned the thoughts of many of his hearers immediately to Gentiles and to the Romans in particular. But there are enough examples given in the Gospels to let us know that Jesus himself did not exclude either Gentiles (the Syro-Phonecian woman whose daughter was possessed by an evil spirit) or the Romans (the Centurion whose servant was dying). One might argue that the few times we see Jesus interacting with Gentiles are merely exceptions and that in general he opposed fraternizing with Gentiles. That argument is hard to maintain, though, in the face of the events that followed the death, resurrection, and ascension of Jesus. The church of the first century A.D. quickly embraced Gentile believers and, in a few decades was more Gentile than Jewish. So Jesus must have had some group, other than Gentiles, in mind when he spoke of "dogs" and "pigs."

I believe he was using the stereotypical image of dogs and pigs as creatures, more concerned with consumption of that which filled their bellies than with an appreciation of culture or sacred things, to indicate the kind of humans whose god is their belly, who as readily bite the hand giving them food as eat the food itself. Certainly Romans, and other Gentiles, fit that description, but so did many Jews, not the least, the ever-present Pharisees. Likely, a large part of the crowd listening to his sermon fit that description. They would prove his words true a few months later as they turned on him and joined the crowd crying out for his crucifixion.

Because Jesus knew the hearts of men much of his preaching consisted of parables. Those, truly hungry for spiritual food, could comprehend his meaning, but the "dogs" and "pigs" would merely sniff at it and turn away in disgust. Jesus came, by his own testimony, "so the world might be saved through him." But even the Son of God could not make disciples of "dogs" and "pigs". Those of us who bear his message to the world should not assume that we are any more persuasive than our Lord was.

Time is precious; it should not be wasted on futile causes. We are called at all times to *be* witnesses of the Gospel, living our lives in ways that show us to be citizen of the kingdom of heaven. On many occasions we will be called, additionally, to *give* witness, declaring that the kingdom of heaven has come. But there are also times to withhold our sacred testimony; to *not* cast our pearls before pigs and dogs, because the dogs and pigs are too blind to comprehend their value.

We should not, however, cease to love those who reject, or even snarl at the Gospel. Instead we should pray, "Thy kingdom come, thy will be done, on earth – in the hearts and minds of "dogs" and "pigs" – as it is in heaven."

Chapter 21

Ask, Seek, Knock

When Jesus says, "Ask and it will be given to you; seek and you will find, knock and the door will be opened to you." it sends every commentator scrambling. "Wait a minute," we say, "I've seen a lot of asking go unanswered, many seekers left still seeking, and plenty of knockers to whom the door was not opened."

The Sermon on the Mount is not the only place where we are told that Jesus made these sweeping promises of answer to prayer. He tells his disciples on another occasion, "Ask anything in my name and it will be given to you."

So what are we to do when we have asked and seemed not to have been given what we asked for? What are we to think when our seeking leaves us still bewildered and lost? What are we to say when we've knocked our knuckles bare and the door is still shut?

A lot of answers to this knotty problem have been offered. Some say that not all answers come in this lifetime; for some we'll need to wait until we reach our eternal home. Another explanation offered is that answers do not always take the form we expected; if we look at our situation from the right perspective we'll see that our prayers were answered. Those who wish to make us feel especially good tell us that God's answers often take the form of "No!" Just as we expect our

85

children to accept a sovereign, "No" from us, we should be willing to accept one from our Heavenly Father. Still others "encourage us" with the opinion that our lack of faith has delayed the answer; if we only bolster our faith we'll see the answers come. And there are those who tell us to just hang on to our hope; that with God a year is as a thousand, and a thousand years is as one. If we have patience we'll see the answer to our prayers. Still others tell us that the kind of miraculous answer to prayer that Jesus talked about came only in apostolic days; that we cannot expect God to intervene miraculously in our day.

That, of course, does not exhaust the explanations given when prayers go, or seem to go, unanswered. All of those listed, and many more that could be added to the list, are credible to greater or lesser degrees under certain circumstances. But Jesus did not give conditions under which prayers would or would not be answered. He stated flatly that they would be answered. I have contended that Jesus meant what he said in this, and in the other parts of the Sermon on the Mount so, when I pray, and the prayer goes unanswered, I cannot simply shrug it off; I need an explanation that leaves Jesus' credibility intact.

My explanation may not satisfy others any more than those offered above satisfy me, but I'll offer it because I believe it does, in fact, maintain the credibility of Jesus' offer to his disciples, and further gives us an understanding of the power available to believers.

Jesus indicated that the things he did, his disciples would do also. Indeed they would do greater things. (That would be a discussion for another time, but not now.) Jesus further indicated in a variety of statements that the things he did were those that he saw his father doing. I believe, by implication, he was saying that he did nothing but what he saw his father doing. The key to his miracles then was not that he possessed special powers as the Son of God in the flesh, but in the fact that he was "binding on earth, what he saw bound in heaven." Or to put it another way, he was praying, with full understanding of God's will, "your will be done on earth as it is in heaven." So, when Jesus told his disciples, "Whatever you ask, *in my name*, it will be given you," he was not giving them a blank check with which to buy condos and Cadillacs, but telling them, "If you ask the Father for anything *you know I would ask of Him*, it will be given you." Likewise, in the Sermon on the Mount, when he says, "Ask and it will be given to you, seek and you shall find, knock and the door will be opened to you." he is revealing to his disciples the power that is theirs if they learn to pray within the Father's will.

And how do we know the Father's will? In the same way Jesus, as son of man, knew it; through study of the Word of God, observation of the world around him, and reliance upon the Spirit of God that indwelt him. Oh, and one more thing, perhaps the thing most likely - in its absence - to hinder our prayers today, *total submission to the will of the Father*.

So, what sounds, at first, like a wonderful offer of

anything and everything one might wish, turns out to be an invitation to submit ourselves to the will of God and become channels through which His will can be done, on earth as it is in heaven.

Chapter 22

The Golden Rule

Why do I feel like running the other way when I see a business sign that incorporates the golden rule?

Golden Rule Used Cars

Is it that I sense that "the lady doeth protest too much?" Yes, I think that is it.

NPR's *Car Talk* hosts, Click and Clack, the Tappet Brothers, tell us, with almost no subterfuge, that their law firm is Dewey, Chetum, and Howe. If I'm dealing with a crook I like to know it right from the start. It is disappointing, to say the least, to find that what you thought was an honest enterprise has lifted your wallet. But most disturbing of all is to be drugged, mugged, and left broke by a business called *Golden Rule Care Givers*.

No principle (or call it commandment if you wish) makes more sense, is more easily remembered, and more universally approved than The Golden Rule. Jesus is not the only religious teacher to propound it. Confucius and Gautama Buddha and others have offered their version of the Golden Rule.

Jesus said of it, ". . . this sums up the Law and the Prophets." That is a very sweeping statement. In other words, by doing to others as you would have them do to you, you will have answered the requirements of the Ten Commandments, the regulations of Jewish Law, and avoided all the sins denounced by the Prophets. Want an easy way to heaven? Here's one.

Well, not quite. It is a marvelous statement of our obligation to each person with whom we have contact. (Don't forget that God is a Person.) But we know that, like all other "Rules for Moral Living," this one is impossible for sinful men and women to faithfully execute on a day to day basis. So, what are we to do?

I've mentioned elsewhere a motto invented by one of the participating teams in a mock United Nations session to which I took some students years ago. Sensing that their project was not the equal of some of the others, they declared that they were operating under the principle that, "If it is worth doing, it is worth doing poorly."

Perhaps our attitude toward the Golden Rule should be, "If it is worth living by, it is worth living by poorly." If we wait to attempt moral living until we can do it perfectly we will make no progress toward Christ-likeness in our lives. And worse, we will make no impression, for good, upon those we are sent to be witnesses to.

"Is that what we are supposed to do; show off our righteousness?" you ask. Yes, in a sense, different than the exhibitionism of the Pharisees, we are to do good works so that those watching our lives will glorify our Father in heaven. The mere fact that our goal is to glorify the Father, and not to display our righteousness, will temper our tendency to self-aggrandizement.

Thankfully, our standing before God is not determined by our perfect observance of the Golden Rule, but by Jesus' sacrifice for our sins. With the issue of our standing before the Father settled by our faith in Christ, we are set free to begin to live, with the assistance of the Holy Spirit, like a member of God's family. And there is no better guide to that kind of living than the Golden Rule.

Chapter 23

Obeying the Signs

The sign read, "Enter through the narrow gate." But the crowd was headed for the other gate, the wide one. What to do? The object was to get in and it surely looked like the majority had figured out that the quickest and most pain-free way was through the wide gate.

There were advantages to going to the narrow gate; fewer people crowded that path. The debris from discarded litter was not as prevalent. Actually, although the path was narrow, as was the gate itself, those on that path were less rude and pushy. In addition, there seemed to be little if any backup at the gate itself. Of course if everyone suddenly decided to go that way there would be an awful crush of humanity.

And besides, there must be some reason the crowds were going the other way; going enthusiastically actually, pushing and shoving each other in their hurry to "get in." Most seemed happy but there were occasional altercations when someone thought another person was pushing ahead in the line.

When faced with a situation like this we quickly learn what kind of person we are. The sign after all read, "Enter through the narrow gate." So why would a nice person like you – like me – not obey the sign? Well, for many reasons, perhaps the most common being that we are influenced by the crowd. But there is also a sort of rebellion against being told there is only one way to get in. Some bureaucrat, no doubt, is trying to decide for other people what is best for them. Or, it could be a trick too; a way to siphon off part of the crowd into some less desirable area. Who wants to get stuck with all those suckers who headed for the narrow gate? And besides, even if the wide gate proves to be the wrong choice, there will surely be a way to get around to the area that the narrow gate leads to.

Near the end of the Sermon on the Mount Jesus said to the crowd:

> Enter through the narrow gate. For wide is the gate and broad is the road that leads to destruction, and many enter through it. But small is the gate and narrow the road that leads to life, and only a few find it.

Those are among the most daunting words Jesus spoke while he was on earth. The instruction is clear. The choice is unequivocal. The consequences of the choice are certain and irreversible. It is, as clearly as any choice can be, a matter of life and death.

What is it that Jesus is describing in these stark terms? What do these gates open into? He tells us. One leads to life, one to destruction – death. But the hearer must take it on faith that Jesus knows what he is saying. Only after one is through the gate – which ever gate one chooses – and it has swung shut behind him or her, does one know for sure if Jesus words are true.

It is not God's will that the road to life be so sparsely traveled, but he knows the mind and heart of man. Only a few will find it. That idea runs contrary to the belief of our time. In our U.S. culture, the majority of adults declare themselves on the road to life. Jesus says otherwise. And sadly the evidence points otherwise as well.

In the earlier parts of the Sermon on the Mount Jesus has been describing the road to life. It is progressively narrowed by the requirements Jesus lays down regarding life in the kingdom of heaven. As beautiful as the beatitudes may sound on first hearing, they become more and more onerous to those whose hearts are wedded to the kingdom of this world as they hear the elaboration of what it means to be a citizen of the kingdom of Christ. The broader road looks better to more and more people, and the crowd drifts to the wide gate.

And who is left traveling the narrow road to the narrow gate? Those who are poor in spirit, meek, merciful, peace makers, hungry and thirsty for righteousness, pure in heart, persecuted for righteousness sake. To those on the broad road they seem a pathetic crowd; fools, actually, who deserve the ridicule of all who travel the broad road. But in the end the narrow gate opens into eternal life.

The broad road? Where does it lead? Well, let's just say that Jesus warned us to enter through the narrow gate. He not only warns us; he *invites* us to enter.

Chapter 24

Wise Men and Foolish Men

There are actually very few complete sermons presented in the New Testament, perhaps none, really. But there are summaries that seem to give us a "complete" outline of a particular sermon. Such is the case with the Sermon on the Mount. Jesus, and those who heard him preach on that occasion, expended considerable energy traveling from all over Israel and the surrounding regions to the site of the sermon. Since they labored up a mountain to find a *topos*, a place where the sermon could be delivered, it is inconceivable that the it would last only the ten minutes or less that Matthew's account would seem to indicate. More likely Jesus was "teaching" rather than orating and the event undoubtedly consumed much the day. If Matthew had recorded the full text of what Jesus said, even fewer people would read it today than have read his short version over the years.

But Matthew's account is complete enough to give us a clear picture of what Jesus taught about the kingdom of heaven in that sermon. And then Matthew gives us Jesus' conclusion to the sermon: (emphases added)

> Therefore *everyone who hears these words* of mine *and puts them into practice* is like a wise man who built his house on the rock. The rain came down, the streams rose, and the winds blew and beat against that house, yet it did not fall, because *it had its foundation on the rock*. But everyone who hears these words of mine and

> does not put them into practice is like a foolish
> man who built his house on sand. The rain came
> down, the streams rose, and winds blew and beat
> against that house, and if fell with a great crash.

In this brief conclusion, Jesus reveals his expectation for the "use" of the Sermon on the Mount. He emphasized the need for *orthopraxis*, i.e. "right-doing." The Pharisees, and the teachers of the Law were long on external practice, particularly public practice. The principles of the kingdom of heaven that Jesus had been expounding, if practiced, would have public (societal) implications and manifestations, but they were mostly practices of the heart. Jesus came to change the heart of man, knowing that a change of heart means a change of behavior. Someone has said that orthodoxy (right-believing) leads to orthopraxis.

However, it is not a given that *right-believing* will invariably lead to *right-doing*. Even a true change of heart still leaves one with choices to make – a life to live – a "house" to build. The house begun with enthusiasm and faith will not stand the wear and tear of storms and floods if it is not built upon a firm foundation. Jesus told his audience, "This – these words I've spoken to you – these principles of kingdom living – is the rock upon which you can build a house that will endure."

Think of it; in the Sermon on the Mount, Jesus has been describing the building blocks of a solid and lasting Christian life. In the beatitudes, he described the *character* of the citizen of the kingdom of heaven. In his analogy of salt and light, he portrayed the disciple's *mission* in the world at large. In a series of "you have heard it said, but I say" statements, he explained the believer's *relationship to God's commandments*. And finally, he tells the disciple's their *attitude toward others* in the kingdom is to be non-judgmental.

That is the way God intended mankind to live, and had he lived that way there would have been no "fall" and no need for a Savior. Sadly, however, fallen man, though he knows the way to live, finds he cannot consistently live that way. His best righteousness turns out to be inadequate to save him. God, in mercy, provided for that shortfall in righteousness through the redemptive death of Christ on the cross. That is the good news of the kingdom of God. All who place their faith in Christ can have the *everlasting life* that Adam jettisoned through his rebellion.

But the "bad news" of the kingdom of heaven is that we are still expected, despite the redemptive work of Christ on our behalf, to live by the principles of the kingdom of heaven taught in the Sermon on the Mount and elsewhere. Our daily prayer is to be that God's will will be done on earth as it is in heaven.

But the "good news" – to put one final twist on the "bad news/good news" theme – is that Jesus promised his disciples that he would send an *ezer*, a *paraclete*, a helper (the Holy Spirit) to remind them of the things he had taught them, and help them to be good citizens of the kingdom of heaven.

Only the very foolish build on sand, Yet there are those today who resist building on the teachings of the Sermon on the Mount, which Jesus called the rock on which a lasting "house" can be built. They view the "moral teaching of Jesus" as a dangerous path to a "bloodless" redemption – "mere works" – attempting to please God by being "nice people."

It is just as foolish, in my view, to believe that the house can be built without "right-doing" as it is to believe that "right-doing" alone can build it. Only those who have placed their whole faith in Christ's redemptive life and death and resurrection will even begin to build the house. But those who imagine that having placed their faith in Christ's redemptive work, exempts them from the need to build upon the rock of Jesus' teachings, are building on sand – precious blood-stained sand for sure – but sand nonetheless, and Jesus said the storms will wash away what they have built.

Chapter 25

Amazed, But Uncommitted

How do we account for the fact that the huge crowd that heard Jesus' Sermon on the Mount left "amazed at his teaching," in Matthew's words, but three years later only a handful of women, and possibly one apostle, stood within sight of the cross upon which he was being crucified?

Matthew concludes his description of the Sermon on the Mount with these words:

> When Jesus had finished saying these things, the crowds were amazed at his teaching, because he taught as one who had authority, and not as their teachers of the Law.

It is easy to misconstrue Matthew's words and probably his intent, too. I believe most of us have done so at times. We can easily believe that he is saying, "The people left, eager and excited to try out their new 'rules for living.' They immediately became the community of saints that Jesus indicated should inhabit the kingdom of heaven. When confronted with insults they turned the other cheek. When asked to lend their cloak they offered their coat too. When required to go a mile they gladly went two. They became peacemakers in their communities." In other words, like the wise man building his house on the rock, they *put in practice* the words that Jesus had taught them.

Probably not!

You see, Matthew did not say the crowds eagerly sought to become the kind of people Jesus portrayed as kingdom people. He said they were amazed at the *authority* with which Jesus taught them. In other words they had heard a man who not only talked straight; he taught with the authority of one who knew what he was talking about. The crowd did not know that he had spent the night before in prayer to his Heavenly Father, but they sensed that there was something radically different in this man than what they heard each week in their synagogue. They were excited, perhaps expectant that Jesus might at last be that Messiah for whom they wished. They may even have been ready to accept a call to arms. But to "lay down their arms," to "turn the other cheek," to "love their enemies"? Not yet. Not this crowd.

Here, I think, we see part of the reason for the resistance to the Sermon on the Mount that I've noted over the years. The Jews who heard Jesus that day were excited by a man who "says it like it is," very likely believing he would create the kind of kingdom on earth that they envisioned. They would, over the next three years, see that Jesus was serious about the kingdom he described in the Sermon on the Mount, and not at all interested in the kingdom they so ardently desired.

A winnowing would have to occur, a dying, not just of the Messiah, but also of the aspirations of those who would be his disciples. "If any *man* will come after me, let him deny himself, and take up his cross daily, and follow me," Jesus said. Those willing to "die" and be raised again with him, would then truly "hunger and thirst" for the kingdom of righteousness he had described to them. They would be eager for the image of Christ to be formed in them by the Spirit that he would send them.

When I see the multitudes that now flock to Christian meetings around the world, I have to think of that crowd on the mountain side. And I ask, "Do they hunger and thirst for the kingdom Jesus offers, or do they envision a Messiah who will establish a kingdom of their liking; one built on the principles of this world? Are they committed to the principles of the kingdom of heaven, or are they enamored with the apparent 'success' of the movement they are witnessing. Do they hunger and thirst for the righteousness the Spirit of God wants to build in them, or will they walk away when they learn that following Christ means entering into his suffering and bearing his cross daily? Is the way still straight and the gate still narrow that leads to eternal life? Are there still few who find it?"

I've been using "they" in the previous paragraph but it should be "I", because the message of this powerful sermon is as personal as any can be. The Sermon on the Mount narrows the focus not to one nation, not to one religion, or one denomination. Not even to one congregation. It narrows it to one person. What kingdom am *I* longing for – committed to? Would I prefer some kingdom other than that which Jesus declared was "at hand"? Am I willing to have the Spirit of God create in me the "fruit" appropriate for a citizen of the kingdom of heaven?

The answers to those questions determines whether I will simply be "amazed" at the message of the kingdom, or committed to it; whether I will seek some sort of sand on which to build my house, or build it on the rock of Jesus' teaching.

Chapter 26

Concluding Remarks on the Sermon on the Mount

If we had been among the crowd that descended from the mountain after hearing Jesus' teaching in what we now call "the Sermon on the Mount," we would have, lingering in our memory, Jesus final words:

> Therefore everyone who hears these words of mine and puts them into practice is like a wise man who built his house on the rock. The rain came down, the streams rose, and the winds blew and beat against that house; yet it did not fall because it had its foundation on the rock. But everyone who hears these words of mine and does not put them into practice is like a foolish man who built his house on sand. The rain came down, the streams rose, and the winds blew and beat against that house, and it fell with a great crash.

Jesus did not ask for a commitment, on anyone's part, to "practice" what he had preached; he simply stated the consequences of practicing or failing to practice. It was a simple matter of building for success or building for failure. So we would be free, along with the rest of the multitude, to go our way and be whatever kind of person we wished to be. We could build houses on the rock or on the sand, as we wished.

The sad truth is that the human race – the kingdom of this world – has chosen to build on the sand, ignoring the things that Jesus said would bring "blessedness" and permanence to their lives. The result has been two thousand years of collapsing houses. The even sadder truth is that within the church that bears the name of Christ, his teachings have been marginalized as well. No one I know would overtly say that one should practice behaviors in direct contravention of Jesus' teaching, although many (perhaps all of us at times) squirm and seek to find reasons why Jesus didn't mean his words to be taken literally.

But the bigger issue raised by the Sermon on the Mount relates to its purpose within the whole body of Christian theology and praxis. Was Jesus offering a path to redemption through right-behavior? Some – particularly liberal theologians of the 19th and early 20th century – as a child I heard them roundly and regularly denounced as "modernist" preachers – seem to be saying that he was; that the kingdom of this world could be transformed into the kingdom of God if humankind would only attend to the words of Jesus in the Sermon on the Mount and elsewhere. They discounted, and in some instances outright rejected, the death of Christ as an atonement for the sins of mankind. Faith in Christ, to them, simply meant a belief in, and a sincere attempt to live by the principles he taught and demonstrated during his life on earth.

It is my contention that – if I may borrow an analogy from Luther – much of the Fundamentalist / Evangelical Christian church has *fallen off the other side of the horse* in an attempt not to associate themselves with a "works-based" salvation. But in the process they have created what some have

termed "cheap grace." Faith in the atoning work of
Christ is, for them, the sole criteria by which one's
salvation is achieved. They would never say this,
but their position suggests that they believe it would
be nice if people lived by the principals that Jesus
taught, but their doing so or not doing so is
irrelevant to their standing before God.

And thus both have widened the gate and broadened
the path that Jesus declared was straight and
narrow. Liberal theology has failed to produce a
perfect works-based society. Evangelicalism, on the
other hand, has succeeded in creating a massive,
world-wide, grace-based movement. Evangelical
Grace 1, Liberal Theology 0! But no one wins when
the Gospel is distorted in either direction. Souls
hang in the balance and it is incumbent upon the
Church of Jesus Christ to "get it right."

As is so often the case, a middle way is needed.
God has provided a way back to right relationship
with Him through the sacrificial death of his Son. It
is a bloody way that many may find hard to accept,
but the teaching of Scripture and the words of Jesus
himself indicate that there is no other way to the
Father except through His Son. But, to return to the
Father through the gracious gift of the Son's death,
and then to ignore the words of the Son is to walk
away from the very salvation one has just claimed.
That is why Scripture is plain in its description of
those non-kingdom-like behaviors that will prevent
one from entering (or remaining in) the kingdom of
heaven. If Jesus is the King, those who wish to live
in his kingdom had better be willing to live by the

principles of his kingdom. Not always *able to do so*, but *willing*.

Is the King gracious? Yes, he knows we are a work in progress. Is he patient? Yes, he has granted me long years, and still is working to instruct me. Does he demand instant perfection? Obviously, no. But what he does ask is a poverty of spirit and a hunger and thirst for righteousness. And even those, we cannot claim to be of our doing; his Spirit is building them in the believer, bit by bit.

The Sermon on the Mount provides a partial description (it is only one of Jesus' discourses) of the kingdom of heaven. The Epistles reiterate and expand upon the picture given in the Gospels. Together they give us a blueprint, so to speak, for building that house that will last through eternity. The building permit, we pick up at the cross. If we walk away from the cross and never start to build the house it can be questioned whether we have even become Disciples of Christ. But if we try to build the house, and attempt to do so without reference to the blueprint, as one "who hears these words of mine and does not put them into practice;" if we choose to build on sand, rather than the rock, the house "**will fall with a great crash**."

There are only two possible outcomes for a human life. Either the "house" we build will endure, or be destroyed. Those outcomes are indicated in two phrases Jesus used in teaching about the importance of finishing well. In one scenario we will hear, "Well done, good and faithful servant. Enter into the joy of your Lord." In the other we will hear, "I never knew you; depart from me."

About that Cover Drawing

I would so like to give credit to the young man who drew the caricature of me in 1969 that appears on the back cover of this book. I can only guess at the signature in the lower right hand corner of the drawing. He was a student at Stillwater, MN High School during the year that I served as an intern on the World History team there. He captured everything so beautifully from my wingtip shoes to my slicked down hair and sideburns, the formal coat and tie, and the ever-present grade book. My only objection is that I know I must have looked much younger then than his drawing makes me appear. Today, of course, I look much older.

James Rapp, November 2013

www.ingramcontent.com/pod-product-compliance
Lightning Source LLC
Chambersburg PA
CBHW071901020426

42331CB00010B/2623